Four Hundred Years of Music Printing

A. HYATT KING

Four Hundred Years of Music Printing

Published by the Trustees of the British Museum: London 1964

List of Illustrations

'or permission to reproduce plates III, IV, IX, X, XI, and XIII
hanks are due to the libraries named in each entry. All the other
•lates are reproduced from books in the collections of the British
Museum.

The measurements, in centimetres, given in the caption to each plate, are those of the full page of the copy photographed.

Preface

The art of printing books from movable type was invented by Johann Gutenberg at Strassburg c. 1436–39, perfected by him at Mainz in 1450–55, and spread during the 1460s to the cities of northern and central Italy. From c. 1473 onwards, the main streams of music-printing rose, broadly speaking, in the same parts of Europe and flowed thence throughout the western world.

In this booklet I have described how the four chief processes – printing from movable type, from blocks of wood or metal, from engraved plates and by lithography – gradually developed in relation to the art of music itself. I have outlined their evolution and use down to the introduction of machine-printing in the later part of the nineteenth century. My account is mostly restricted to countries in or near the main stream – Germany, Italy, France, England and the Netherlands. I have also mentioned the principal landmarks of music-printing in the Americas. Because this booklet is intended primarily for English readers, I have given some prominence to developments in England.

Music Room
The British Museum

A. HYATT KING

Four Hundred Years of Music Printing

The printing of music differs essentially from the printing of a purel
verbal text. As this difference arises from the divergence betwee
the nature of music and the nature of literature, it must be sum
marised at the outset. Whereas in a verbal text the letters forming
word represent a concept to be conveyed by the eye to the brain, i
music the note, whether accompanied by a text or not, is primaril
an instruction to bring into action lungs or fingers, or both com
bined, in order to produce a sound at a certain pitch and of a certai
duration. Besides devising symbols to convey these instructions wit
unmistakable precision, the musical typographer has also to bear i
mind the need to indicate as clearly as possible, first, the interval
of whatever degree, between the pitch of one note and that of th
next, and second, the changes in spacing between one note or grou
of notes, and the next, as required by changes in time-values. Thes
are principles of horizontality.

The vertical principle is equally important, and is likewise on
that hardly arises in the printing of words. Two or more notes ma
need to be printed on one or more staves, in exact vertical align
ment, in order to produce the simultaneous sound known as a chord
In vocal works, a precise vertical relationship has also to be estab
lished between the notes on the stave and the syllables of th
underlying text. Because, moreover, in performance music is usuall
placed further away from the eye than is the text of a book whe
being read, the factors of distance and proportion produce speci
problems of design. All these essentials are closely inter-related, an
are peculiar to the nature and purpose of musical notes, whethe
they are to be printed from movable type or by any other proces
Consequently, their design, shape, and spacing on the page ar
much more complex than those of the letters of a word.

The early history of printing, from about 1450 to the end of th
year 1500, is usually known as the period of 'incunables', a ter
derived from the Latin word 'incunabulum', which means a crad

nd hence the first beginnings of the art. It was during this time, when the printing of books soon reached a high level of technical excellence often combined with great beauty of design, that the printing of music began. However tentative or clumsy these beginnings may seem, it should be remembered that, as with books, so with music, the printer strove to reproduce mechanically the style of the best manuscripts.

This incunable period was also one of the most momentous in musical history, marked by great strides – especially at the Burgundian court and in Italy – in the skill of composing polyphonic music. But the printing of such compositions, elaborate as they were in rhythm and notation, posed problems that baffled the early printers, even after they had mastered the technique of fitting notes on to staves in the liturgical books on which their efforts in the field of music were mainly concentrated. They also produced books dealing with various aspects of theory and instruction, many of which required short musical examples. In order to reproduce these, the printers generally used blocks, mostly of wood, sometimes perhaps of metal. For music in liturgies, however, they preferred movable type. Before 1501, nearly 270 liturgies with music appeared, and about a score of books containing musical examples. But not one book of polyphonic compositions came from any press anywhere in Europe.

This preponderance of liturgy was due to universal demand and to the fact that, compared with polyphony, its music was simple, consisting almost entirely of plainsong, which was monophonic and so restricted in range that it rarely exceeded the compass of a stave of four or five lines. Because its notes had few variations in time-value, the basic forms of their physical shapes likewise varied little. Thus the problem of designing and casting the music types was limited from the outset.

In the process of making these types (as for letters) the essential instrument was a metal mould, cased in wood as a protection against heat, and opening on a hinge. The base was formed by the matrix, a piece of metal into which the outline of the note or note-group had been struck by a punch bearing the design cut in high relief. Molten type-metal, probably lead alloyed with tin and antimony, was then poured into the mould, from which, after setting quickly, it was extracted as a stick bearing the note-shape on its working end.

(This process, with the necessary changes in the design and size of the punches, also served to produce types for printing mensural music, in which the relative note-values were precisely indicated. Initially, the process was simplified by the fact that by the mid fifteenth century, only two styles of plainsong notation were in general use, both derived in simplified forms from those of liturgical manuscripts. The Germanic parts of Europe preferred a 'Gothic' form (PL. I and II); in Latin countries, England and parts of the Netherlands, a 'Roman' form, which was usually square (PL. III and IV), prevailed.

Even after the music-type had been cast, the technical problems were still very great. The printer had to devise a system for correlating staves, notes and text. (This was made easier if, as not infrequently happened, either the space for the staves was left blank and the lines were ruled by hand, or the notes were so added on a printed stave.) Using for the staves a block of metal or occasionally separate lengths of rules, the printer set this material together with the words of the text in the forme, and printed both at the first impression. He then removed all this type from the forme and replaced it with the type required for the second impression. This comprised the clefs, and the notes set with such meticulous spacing that each would leave its impression right on the centre of the appropriate line of the stave, and stand in an equally exact vertical relation to the syllables of the text printed beneath. It is in the light of these special problems that the notable achievement of successive generations of early printers should be assessed.

It is reasonably certain that the first book of music ever printed is a Gradual, of which the only complete copy extant is in the British Museum. It lacks both a date and a printer's name, but the type used to print the text is identical with that of the 'Constance Breviary', one copy of which was rubricated in 1473. Because the press which used this type had but a short life, the Gradual may be assigned to this year, or a little later. It was printed, if not at Constance, certainly at some town in the southern part of Germany, where the printing of books had begun some twenty years before. The music is printed from movable type in Gothic notation: two pages, showing this and some of the decorative initials which were added in colour by hand, are reproduced as PL. I and PL. II.

The volume which stands second in the history of music printing
joys the distinction of being the first to bear a date. This is a
issal with a full colophon which states that it was printed in Rome
12 October 1476 by Ulrich Han (a native of Ingolstadt). The
usic is printed in Roman notation, with initials in red or blue, and
uches of yellow in the capitals, all added by hand. The layout
d general effect of the page (PL. III) are a good deal clearer than
ose of its German rival. From these beginnings the type-printing
music in liturgies spread quite rapidly through most of Europe
it did not appear in England until 10 January 1500 when Pynson
inted a beautiful Sarum Missal in two colours (PL. IV).

The skill acquired by the early printers was not used with pro-
essive consistency, nor did it undergo much technical develop-
ent. Even in the 1490s, the staves were often left blank for the
otes to be added by hand. Sometimes both staves and notes were
ill so added. The reasons for this were liturgical, economic and
chnical. Music-type was costly and consequently scarce. Its use in
double impression was slow and expensive. Not all those who
inted service books could afford this extra luxury. By no means all
ioceses followed the use of Rome. Local requirements could be met
ore conveniently if the notes, at least, were added by hand. This
abled a printer to find a ready market for the same service book
different parts of Europe. In addition, a printer could not set
usic type without some knowledge of music. Such knowledge was
obably as rare as was that of Greek, the general lack of which had
similarly restricting effect on the setting of Greek texts.

The conservative habit of printers was fortified by the timeless,
nchanging character of plainsong. There is thus often little visual
ifference between a Roman Missal of 1490 and one of 1530. The
ypes and layout used for a book of plainsong printed at, say, Seville
the 1490s are remarkably similar to those found in the Ordinary
inted at Mexico City by Juan Pablos in 1556 – the first music
inted in the New World – from the press which Juan Cromberger
ad sent thither from Spain in 1539. (The music in this Ordinary
as printed in Roman notation, as was also the earliest Christian
usic composed in the New World, namely Juan Navarro's *Liber de
uatuor passiones*, published at Mexico City in 1604.)

For a more progressive approach to the printing of music, we may
urn to those works of theory and the like which were published

1

before 1501. Though they number barely a score, less than on
fourteenth of the total of liturgies, they contain music which, beir
as varied in its range as in its purpose, must have provided
welcome challenge to the printer's skill.

The earliest use of movable type for printing music other than i
liturgies occurs in 1473 when Conrad Fyner of Esslingen printe
five identical square notes in descending sequence to illustrate tl
mystical meaning of certain words in Charlier de Gerson's *Co
lectorium super magnificat*. The importance of this passage has bee
exaggerated. It is little more than a curiosity, devoid of significanc
as music, to which it stands in much the same relationship as woul
the first five letters of the alphabet, if so printed, to the words of
sentence. An expedient similar to Fyner's was devised by Wynky
de Worde in 1495 for the first attempt at printing musical notatic
in England. In his edition of Higden's *Polycronicon* he combine
quads (or perhaps reversed capitals) with rules to print notes an
staves illustrative of the consonances of Pythagoras (PL. va).

We meet the first appearance of a true musical idea on a page c
Franciscus Niger's *Grammatica* (PL. vb) printed at Venice in 148
by Theodor of Würzburg. It occurs in that section of the gramma
which deals with the rhythms of five metres used by various Latï
poets, and shows how the verses were chanted in schools. Th
passage is doubly important as containing the earliest known prin
ing both of secular music and of mensural notes. There is little doul
that the notes were printed from type and not, as some authoritic
believe, from a metal block.[1] The staves were to be added by han
In the second edition of the same work (Basle, c. 1485) the sam
notes are printed from a wood-block, which is thus the first used fc
secular music. More extended use of wood-block is found in Nicolau
Burtius's *Musices opusculum* (Bologna, 1487), which includes what
probably the first printed polyphonic music complete with stave
(PL. via). (Only two liturgies with all the music printed by thi
method are known – an *Obsequiale augustense* (Augsburg, 1487) an
a Roman missal (Speyer, 1493).)

The versatility of the wood-block was proved in various book
with musical examples. In the second part of Gafori's *Practic

[1]Comparison of several copies shows that the measurements of various note
are identical and that in several places there occur under the notes smudges whic
can only have been caused by quads or pieces of metal rising in the forme.

usicae (Milan, 1496), blocks were used for a good many polyphonic uotations. Wood-block likewise served for the earliest printings of ramatic music – the four-part chorus in Veradrus's play *Historia aetica* (Rome, 1493), and the more elaborate choruses in Reuchlin's *cenica progymnasmata* (Strassburg, 1498). What is probably the arliest printed German secular song, found in *Von sant Ursulen hifflin* (Strassburg, 1497), is also reproduced by an unusual use of iis process – the notes (in Gothic form), the staves, and the text all eing cut on wood. This method of music-printing flourished hroughout the first half of the sixteenth century. It was much nproved by Jan de Greet of Antwerp (for the songs in *Lofzangen r eere van keizer Maximilian*, 1515), and reached a high level of rtistry in such a book as the edition of Luther's *Geystliche Lieder* rinted at Leipsic by Valentin Babst in 1545 (PL. VII). No example f wood-block used to print music in England is known from the fteenth century, but a good example from the sixteenth is found in he music of Robert Crowley's Psalter of 1549.

The subsequent history of wood-block may be briefly outlined ere. Although infrequently used after about 1600, it did not die ut for a long time, especially in some places remote from the main- tream of music-printing. In 1698 B. Green and J. Allen of Boston, Iassachusetts, used it for the music in the ninth edition of the Bay 'salm Book. (This is notable as the first music-printing in what is ow the United States.) All the numerous songs in the six volumes f the *Musical Miscellany*, issued by John Watts of London, 1729-31, re neatly cut on wood. In 1754 John Sadler of Liverpool was well erved by finely cut blocks for all the music in a large song-book ntitled *The Muses' Delight*. Blocks were also favoured for printing hort pieces in various literary magazines, and as late as 1843 were ut to a not inelegant use by the Moscow book publisher Auguste emen for the musical examples in Oulibicheff's *Nouvelle biographie e Mozart*. Such instances testify to the lasting value of a process, owever limited in scope, applied to the printing of music over a pan of more than 350 years.

The early development of movable type for mensural music made low progress. After its use in the *Grammatica* of 1480, there is no ther example recorded before its re-appearance in two books which vere printed at Paris by Michel Tholoze, c. 1496. These are an dition of *Musicales regule* (PL. VIb) by Guillermus Guersoni, and an anonymous treatise entitled *L'art et instruction de bien dancer*. I both the design of the mensural types is rough and the handling c them distinctly uncertain. Yet these two books contain the las known use of mensural types before the end of the incunable perioc

In the light of such indifferent craftsmanship, the progress mad by Ottaviano dei Petrucci, barely five years later, is all the mor remarkable. A native of Fossombrone near Pesaro, he came t Venice in 1491 and obtained his exclusive privilege to print musi on 25 May 1498. Possibly for technical reasons connected wit cutting and casting the variety of types required, his first book, th famous *Odhecaton*, was delayed until 14 May 1501. Thus by less tha five months, beyond the arbitrary limit set by posterity, Petrucc failed to qualify as an incunable printer. Consequently, having bee overlooked by specialists in the early history of printing, he has nc received the general recognition that his great technical geniu deserved.

Petrucci's artistic personality as type-cutter and printer breathe on every page that came from his press. He combined notes, rest and directs of an elegant design with a well-aligned text an beautiful but unobtrusive initial letters. The registration of notes o₁ the stave is as perfect as is the spacing of the parts, which are usuall laid out separately on open pages, in the manner of a choir-book He employed a triple impression, printing first the staves, secondl the text, initial letters and signatures, and thirdly the note (PL. VIII). Petrucci also showed the mastery of his art in being th first printer to face and solve the problems of printing lute tablatur (PL. IX). By 1520, when the last of his sixty-one publication appeared, he had made a quantity of music by the great masters o the period more widely available than ever it could have been i₁ manuscript copies.

It was in Petrucci's time that there occurred a remarkable experi ment with a combination of processes, which seems to have had n₁ imitators. In 1515 Petrus Sambonettus of Siena printed a collectio₁ entitled *Canzone, sonetti, strambotti, et frottole*. The music was mos probably printed from metal blocks, and the underlaid text cer tainly from type, both presumably at one impression. Metal-bloc₁ was also most probably used for two remarkable books of orga₁ music, Andrea Antico's *Frottole intabulate da sonare organi* (Rome 1517) and *Recerchari, motetti e canzoni*, composed by Marco Antoni

Cavazzoni, and printed at Venice in 1520 by Bernardus Vercellensis. The latter contains the earliest known use of chords and ties (PL. XIIa), which would have been very difficult to print in this style by any other method.

The sheer perfection of Petrucci's process must have made it slow and costly. Triple impression is rarely found elsewhere. It was most probably used by Peter Schoeffer when he printed Arnolt Schlick's *Tabulaturen etlicher Lobgesang* at Mainz in 1512. Petrucci's method and style were however most widely imitated by various printers, who used only double impression but often with great success. Sigismund Grimm and Marc Wirsung of Augsburg printed Senfl's *Liber selectorum cantionum* as a sumptuous folio in 1520. An unknown printer, working 'at the sign of the Black Morens' in London, produced distinguished work in the famous *XX songes* of 1530. Earlier than these, and less successful, was Erhard Oeglin of Augsburg, who printed Tritonius's *Melopoeiae* in 1507, using short type-segments which gave a rather disjunct effect.

A notable change in style of printing with two impressions was due to the French composer Elzéar Genet, usually called Carpentras, after his birthplace. In 1532 he caused to be published at Avignon, at his own expense, two collections of his sacred compositions, using a beautiful type designed under his supervision by Étienne Briard. The round-headed notes, remarkable as the first of their kind, are based upon the style of contemporary manuscripts. In the 1550s Robert Granjon printed music with small round notes and used 'caractères de civilité' for the text.

As these and other beautiful books of music were issued in small editions, the cost remained high. Economic factors could only be altered by the introduction of a process needing but a single impression. This could be achieved solely by adopting a new typographic principle whereby each note would be cast as a separate unit, with the adjacent portions of the stave attached to the stem and the head of the note. The inventor of this process is unknown. Fournier, in his *Traité de l'imprimerie musicale*, 1763, stated that it was invented by Pierre Haultin of Paris in 1525: this, though long accepted, has recently been doubted.) It was probably first used, however, by the great publisher Pierre Attaingnant, who issued the earliest of his numerous, very important books of chansons and other music on 4 April 1527 (1528) (PL. X). A single impression is also

found in two anonymous pieces of music both printed by Joh
Rastell of London, each of which survives in a unique copy in th
British Museum. These are a fragmentary song for single voice, an
a three-part song 'Tyme to pas with goodly sport', in *A New Interlu*
and a mery the nature of the iiii Elements (PL. XI) written by Raste
himself. Neither bears a date, but both have been tentative
assigned to the years immediately following 1525. Rastell's use
this revolutionary process may therefore be at least as early
Attaingnant's. Its invention marks the beginning of a new era in th
history of music printing, for with various improvements an
modifications, it has remained in use all over Europe ever sinc
though to a steadily diminishing extent.

In its early stages, however, economic and technical gain wa
only won at the expense of clarity and elegance, because the di
junct, uneven appearance of the lines and notes is so clumsy as
recall the faults of the printers working before Petrucci. Th
unevenness remained for over two centuries, although it was som
times reduced by good press-work, as in the best mid-sixteent
century productions of such Venetian printers as Gardano or Scott
or by excellent type-design as found for instance in the notab
part-books printed in the 1570s by Christophe Plantin at Antwer

Even at its best, however, the capacity of music printing in th
tradition soon began to lag behind the rapid development
musical styles and forms. In the second half of the sixteenth centur
tablature was already obsolescent. A little later, the rise an
dominance of the Italian aria, the birth of opera and other larg
scale vocal forms, made the printing of music in score a genera
necessity. While counterpoint became less elaborate, the growth
the florid style in music for keyboard solo and for stringed instru
ments introduced quicker tempi and more varied rhythms, whic
needed an ever-increasing variety of sorts for their representation i
print. Movable type, used at a single impression, proved sufficient
adaptable to meet the simpler needs of these and other develop
ments in musical history for another century and a half. But th
technical limitations of the process became more and more obviou
and though it was less costly and laborious than double impressio
it was bound to remain slow.

Clearly the printer needed an entirely different, more flexib
process. This was found by gradually adapting to the special requir

PLATE I. The earliest known book of printed music. Printed from type, the notes in Gothic notation, by double impression, with rubricated initials added by hand. The 'Constance' Gradual. [*Southern Germany? Constance?* c. 1473]; fol. 1 recto (30·8 × 22·0 cm)

PLATE II. The earliest known book of printed music. Printed from type, the notes in Gothic notation, by double impression, with rubricated initials added by hand. The 'Constance' Gradual. [*Southern Germany? Constance?* c. 1473]; fol. 56 verso (30·8 × 22·0 cm)

ents of music the use of engraved copper plates. Although this
rocess had been invented in the early fifteenth century, its earliest
nown application to music did not occur until 1581 when Giorgio
Marescotti of Florence printed the first edition of Galilei's *Dialogo
. . della musica antica e della moderna*. All the musical examples in
his book are type-set except two, on p. 71 and p. 78, each of which
printed from an engraved plate. The latter (PL. xiib) consists of
table showing the finals and dominants of the twelve modes. Just
s one hundred years before, the beginnings of mensural music
rinting occurred in a theoretical work, so it was another such book
hat initiated the revolutionary process which had such far-reaching
nd enduring effects.

The skill of engraving had already been perfected in the service
f the visual and graphic arts and of map-making. There was there-
ore no need of a period of experimental groping, such as had marked
he infancy of movable music-type, before its finished mastery could
e applied to music. The first complete engraved compositions seem
ot to have been intended primarily for performance, but, with one
xception, were written specifically for inclusion in a number of
rints made after a drawing or painting of a devotional character
nd issued in the cause of the Counter Reformation. In all of them,
he music is being sung, or sometimes played, by saints or angels,
om open part-books which form an attractive element in the
esign. Although the size of the notes is small, the music is correct
nd legible.

The two earliest prints were both produced at Antwerp, in 1584
nd 1585, engraved by J. Sadeler after Martin de Vos. That of 1584,
epresenting the Virgin and Child with St. Anne (PL. xiii),
ncludes a motet 'Ave gratia plena' by Cornelius Verdonck. The
eissue of this print at Rome in 1586 and again at Antwerp in 1587
uggests that this combination of music and religious art served a
ood purpose as religious propaganda. Of eight similar single-sheet
ngravings issued during the next few years, one was printed at
rankfort on the Main, and one at Mainz. The others bear no place
f imprint but are probably of Flemish origin, because the artists,
omposers and engravers were all of this nationality. Some of the
omposers are known only from these engravings.

The last, and in some respects, the most elaborate of these
picture-motets' appeared about 1590 as the titlepage to a sumptuous

work entitled *Encomium musices*. This is a book of eighteen engravings each representing a scene from the Bible and including many players with instruments, issued by Philip Galle at Antwerp. The music o its titlepage, a motet for six voices by Pevernage, shows the opening of six part-books in the same style as the first 'picture-mote' of 1584.

The skill of the engravers was not, however, confined to repro ducing motets displayed in part-books. Such was their adaptabilit that they could with equal ease and accuracy produce musica publications intended for practical use. In 1575 Simon Veroviu came to Rome from 's Hertzogenbosch, and, italianising his name set up as a writing-master and as an engraver and editor c music. In 1586 he issued the two earliest books of engraved musi They were an anthology of three- and four-part canzonetti, entitle *Diletto spirituale* (PL. XIV), and the *Primo libro delle melodie spiritua* of Jacob Peetrino. By 1608 Verovio had published a dozen engrave books, mostly anthologies, in a very distinctive style. He sometim employed as his engraver a compatriot named Martin van Buytei whose share in the work may, however, have been confined to th titlepages. Verovio's tradition was carried on in Rome by Nicol Borbone, who issued some magnificent volumes of Frescobaldi keyboard music from 1615 onwards. Borbone likewise employed northerner, Christophorus Blancus, a native of Lorraine, as h engraver.

From these and a few other outstanding Italian publications, th engraving of music spread slowly over northern Europe durin the rest of the seventeenth century, during which the printing c music from movable type also flourished as never before. The latte remained the process whereby tens of thousands of instrumental an vocal part-books, large quantities of church music and stage work of every kind (many printed in score) poured from the presses. B about 1700 however engraving had gained the ascendancy in mo of the chief cities of Europe. Despite a limited revival of typ printing towards the middle of the eighteenth century, and agai in the late 1820s, the use of engraved plates predominated right u to the 1870s. The competitive growth of the two processes and the alternate expansion and contraction in different countries make difficult to isolate one from the other. They can perhaps best be see as rivals in a kind of leap-frog race, straggling over most of the ne:

three hundred years, with the invention and application of lithography entering as a *tertius gaudens,* so to speak, in the final stages.

Outside Italy, the first country in which engraved music appeared was England where William Hole, a member of a noted family of engravers and author of a writing-book, prepared for Dorothy Evans of London, *Parthenia,* an anthology of virginal music by Byrd, Bull and Orlando Gibbons. This famous book can be dated between November 1612 and February 1613 from the fact that it was published to celebrate the betrothal of Princess Elizabeth, daughter of James I, to Prince Frederick, Elector Palatine of the Rhine. The style of the engraving is very distinguished (PL. XV). *Parthenia* was followed in November 1613 by Angelo Notari's *Prime musiche nuove,* also engraved by Hole. Holland's turn came next. Before 1620, Joannes Janssen of Amsterdam published several books of lute music in tablature, composed by Nicolas Vallet, the earliest being the *Paradisus musicus testudinis,* engraved by Joannes Berwinckel in 1615, with small but exquisite initials.

Meanwhile, movable type was being put to new and sometimes ingenious musical uses. One of the most distinctive was the so-called 'table-book' in which several parts were printed on two open pages so as to face performers seated at different sides of a table. In 1538 Jacques Moderne of Lyons disposed the four voices of the first book of his *Parangon des chansons* so that they faced in two directions. Later this principle was developed in England so that four-part songs with lute accompaniment were printed to face in three different ways as in Dowland's *First Booke of Songes or Aires* (PL. XVI), printed by Peter Short at London in 1597. (It is interesting to note the parallel between these books and actual tables with surfaces of stone, which were constructed for musical performance during the sixteenth century. The extant specimens are all of German origin and have the parts of complete vocal works etched in relief round their edges and facing outwards towards the singers. Except that the music was not in reverse, these tables anticipate early lithography.)

The credit for producing the earliest known printed musical score belongs to Gardano who so issued in 1577 a collection of madrigals by Cipriano di Rore entitled *Tutti i madrigali a quattro voci spartiti et accomodati per sonar d'ogni sorte l'instrumento perfetto.* These were on four staves. The first surviving opera, Peri's *Euridice* (Marescotti, 1600), was likewise printed in score, mostly on two staves, with five for the choruses. As operatic resources increased, the number of staves used grew to ten or eleven, as found in the later works of Lully.

The music-type generally employed had diamond-shaped lute-heads, with rather short stems. Together with the coarse, broken fragments of the stave attached, this produced a disjunct, unpleasing effect. There were some exceptions, such as the neat, small round-headed notes used by Ballard of Paris for Bataille's *Airs de differents autheurs mis en tablature de luth* in 1608 (PL. XVIIb), a book which is also remarkable as containing possibly the earliest appearance of notes, intended to be sung to one syllable, being tied together by the stems. But the long-lived house of Ballard seldom reached this high standard: as it enjoyed a virtual monopoly for printing music in Paris, it went on using for over two centuries the diamond-shaped notes designed by Guillaume Le Bé as early as 1555. But their employment proved increasingly cumbrous in passages containing many quick notes, which could however be engraved with ease. Thus the score of Colasse's *Thétis et Pélée*, published by Ballard in 1716, used engraved plates for the seventeen pages containing the storm scene, but movable type for the remainder.

Such was Ballard's monopoly that engraving made its way slowly in France. The earliest example known is the *Livre d'orgue* of G. G. Nivers, engraved by Luders in 1667, in a rather heavy style. That of Anglebert's *Pièces de clavecin* of 1689 is a good deal lighter. In Germany too the widespread, generally rather drab use of movable type delayed the introduction of engraving until the second half of the seventeenth century. One of the earliest books is Johann Kuhnau's *Neuer Clavier Übung erster Theil* which the composer engraved himself in 1689. The style is rather thicker than that of English or French engraving, and bears a stronger resemblance to actual handwriting. (This trait is also noticeable later in the case of Telemann, who engraved a few of his own compositions, as possibly did also J. S. Bach.) In 1690 appeared Georg Muffat's *Apparatus musico-organisticus* in which the music is finely engraved throughout. The historiated initial which precedes the opening bars (PL. XVIIa) is one of the most beautiful of its kind, and foreshadows the happy marriage between music-engraving and the visual arts which was to flourish throughout the eighteenth century.

In England during this period there was rather more variety. *Parthenia* was followed by Orlando Gibbons's *Fantasies of III parts*

(c. 1620), *Parthenia in-violata* (c. 1625) and William Childe's exquisitely produced *Psalms* of 1639. After this there was a gap until 1659, when there appeared the first edition of Christopher Simpson's *Division Violist* – another book of florid music. In 1663 William Godbid published the first of several editions of *Musicks Handmaide*. The style and lay-out of this famous book bear some resemblance to those of Purcell's *Sonnatas of III parts* which Thomas Cross engraved so excellently for John Playford and John Carr in 1683. By far the most beautiful English production were the books of violin pieces by Nicola Matteis, engraved by T. Greenhill between about 1675 and 1688. By the 1690s movable type was fighting a losing battle against engraving. Even such a distinguished fount as that cut by the Dutchman Peter de Walpergen for *Musica Oxoniensis*, published by Leonard Litchfield at Oxford in 1698, could not stop the inevitable.

From the time of Verovio onwards, all engraving of music had been done solely on plates of copper, and entirely with engraving tools. As early as about 1660 the punch was in limited use, and soon after 1700 a radical change was introduced, for economic reasons. Instead of copper, which was hard and costly, pewter became general. Being of softer metal, it was easier to work, and the speed of production was increased when the punch partly took the place of the graver. The punch was first used for the heads of the notes, and later for accidentals, clefs, time-signatures, and, in vocal music, for the words of the text. The graver was retained for the stems of the notes, for ties and slurs. The staves were drawn on the plate with a scorer.

The two countries principally concerned in the development of these far-reaching changes were England and Holland. It is uncertain in which they began. Priority seems to belong to Holland where a method of softening copper was discovered towards the end of the seventeenth century, when punching also was practised. Well before 1710 the enterprising Dutch publisher Estienne Roger took full advantage of the new method. His great rival in England was John Walsh the elder, whose first publications, issued from 1696 onwards, were all engraved on copper. The date at which he adopted pewter and punching was probably about 1710. It is noteworthy that not long after this, in 1721, F. Franklin of Boston, Massachusetts, published what was probably the first music printed from engraved plates in the United States – namely Thomas Walter's *The Grounds and Rules of Music explained.*

In France, the engravers clung longer to the materials and style of tradition. Couperin's works engraved by Du Plessy, Mascitti's sonatas by De Baussen, and the posthumous editions of Lully's operas by the latter engraver, are all outstanding productions of the early 1700s. It was not, apparently, until the late 1740s that the use of pewter and punching invaded the world of French music printing. In passing, it may be mentioned that the profession of music-engraver in France could boast throughout the eighteenth century a notable succession of highly skilled women – such as Mlle. Vendôme (later Mme. Moria), Mme. Labassée and Mme. Lobry – unparalleled in other lands.

During most of this period, pure engraving flourished as the process for printing a number of finely illustrated song-books, the best of which rank high among the most elegant works published in any age. The origins of this distinctive genre can perhaps be traced from the Flemish 'picture-motets', through Verovio's decorative pages, to the outstanding historiated initial in Muffat's *Apparatus musico-organisticus*, with a later extension in de Baussen's exquisite scenic illustrations introductory to each act of the late editions of Lully's operas issued c. 1710. In the song-books, the aim of the picture accompanying each piece of music was to represent its mood, place or action.

Again, the art of the writing-master sometimes proved a potent influence. *The Musical Entertainer*, the finest of all the English books (PL. XVIII), was engraved by George Bickham and printed for him in 1737–38. This is a splendid folio. Most of the others, whether issued in England or elsewhere, were small quarto, such as the exquisite *Amaryllis* published by Thomas Jefferys in 1746. The jewe of all the French books is Laborde's *Choix de chansons* (1773) which has brilliant illustrations by J. M. Moreau, each printed, exceptionally, not at the head of each song but on a separate page. (It i curious that the imposition is such that text and illustration are never seen together at a single opening.) The best in German song books is perhaps typified in the *Singende Muse an der Pleisse* (1741) by 'Sperontes' (the pseudonym of J. S. Scholze). The distribution o the ornaments and little figures is most tasteful. Another beautifu German book is J. F. Gräfe's *Oden und Schäfergedichte*, published b

reitkopf in 1744, in which finely engraved headpieces (by Berni-
eroth, father or son) and music are combined with well-spaced text
et in Gothic type below or at the end. A similar combination is
ound in various Dutch song-books of this period.

The early eighteenth century was also notable for the efflorescence
f the dance-book, a type of music printing to which, again, en-
raving was ideally suited. Its remoter ancestry can be seen in the
Balet comique de la royne (Paris, 1582) in which the music was type-set,
nd the beautiful illustrations engraved. A later stage was marked
y Cesare Negri's *Nuove inventioni di balli* (Milan, 1604), in which
tately figures in court costume are illustrated on plates printed
eparately from the pages of the text and music. Among eighteenth
entury books, that which most nearly derives from Negri is perhaps
ambranzi's *Neue und curieuse theatrialische Tantz-Schul* (engraved by
. G. Puschner, Nuremberg, 1721). Each plate, showing grotesque
ancing figures, bears the tune at the foot. A little earlier, in 1700
nd 1706, R. A. Feuillet had issued in Paris two collections of
lances, each showing not the figures but the dainty pattern of the
teps above the tune. A similar combination of decorative dance-
atterns with tunes and figures is found in Kelham Tomlinson's *Art
f Dancing* (London, 1735). Bickham's *Easy Introduction to Dancing*
1738) combines the figure with the music.

During the overwhelming advance of engraving, musical typo-
raphy renewed its forces for what was, as it were, a rearguard
ction. Despite some improvement in the late seventeenth century,
he weakness of movable type lay in its clumsiness and lack of flexi-
ility when used for printing chords and florid music. In the
mid-1740s Johann Gottlob Immanuel Breitkopf began a long period
of research and experiment in order to overcome these limitations.
By 1754 he had perfected a new fount of type of much improved
appearance, and based on a radical departure from the principles
of design that had remained almost unchanged since the days of
Attaingnant. Breitkopf abandoned the idea of a single type-unit
comprising note-head, stem and stave in a single piece. He broke
he unit down into separate pieces for the head and stem, attached
o stave-segments of varying length. He devised another piece that
could be set at the end of the stem, with one, two, or three flags for
he notes in quicker time-values. As his first large work, Breitkopf
printed the score of the pastoral drama *Il Trionfo della fedeltà*,

composed by the Electress Maria Anna Walpurgis of Bavaria, an published it in 1756 under the initials of her pseudonym Ermelind Talia Pastorella Arcada. The use of sharp, well designed type impeccably set, produced a greatly improved appearance (PL. XIX).

During his experiments, Breitkopf had been in regular corre spondence with Pierre Fournier, the great Parisian type-designer who was working along similar lines to improve music-printing The latter's type was even neater than Breitkopf's though perhap less suited to the printing of large scores. It is found at its best in th charming *Anthologie françoise* of Jean Monnet, published by J. G Barbou in 1765. Unfortunately, the monopoly of type-printing held by Ballard prevented the wider use of Fournier's new fount.

Elsewhere in Europe movable type maintained a foothold. In Italy and Spain a considerable amount of music was printed from type which was little changed from the founts used in the mid seventeenth century. But north of the Alps Breitkopf's improvement spread from 1760 onwards with various modifications in style and lay-out, but, on the whole, little improvement. G. L. Winter and J. F. K. Rellstab, both of Berlin, G. L. Hartnoch of Riga, J. J. Lotter of Augsburg, and S. J. Sönnichen of Copenhagen followed Breit kopf's methods but lacked his neatness. In London, however, Henr Fougt, said to have been an immigrant Laplander, printed songs and some sonatas from 1767 to about 1770 in a very neat type likewise clearly based on Breitkopf's, as was also *The Oriental Miscellany*, by W. H. Bird, finely printed at Calcutta in 1789 by Joseph Cooper Here may be mentioned a landmark of this period, the appearance of the first music book printed from movable type in the United States. This was a hymn-book, *Fünff schöne Geistliche Lieder*, issued in Germantown, Maryland, in 1752, by Christoph Saur, who also designed the type.

The fruits of this notable era of experiment were however limited by new forces of musical and social change which gathered strength as the century wore on. From the 1750s concertos and symphonies church music and operas were being composed in ever-increasing quantities, and the numbers needed for their performance were also expanding continually. The large quantity of separate parts required had to be supplied in multiple copies more quickly than was usually possible by the use of movable type or by the employment of hand copyists. A rapid growth of smaller forms, such as chamber music

PLATE III. The second book of printed music and the earliest known bearing a date. Printed from type in Roman notation, by double impression, with initials in red or blue and touches of yellow in some capitals, added by hand. Roman Missal. *Ulrich Han: Rome*, 1476; fol. 120 verso (33·7 × 23·7 cm)

id keyboard solo (where the all-conquering pianoforte rapidly
placed the harpsichord), reflected the rise of a new middle-class
ublic of music-lovers, who required a mass of new music for
omestic performance. All these factors produced an unprecedented
emand for plate-printed music. Throughout Europe, the old-
tablished centres increased their production, and new ones
ompeted with them.

By far the most important was Vienna, where up till about 1775
ery little music had ever been printed. Even so, it is rather curious
nat none of those first active as engravers were native Viennese.
1 1770, three members of the Artaria family from Blevio, on Lake
omo, set up as dealers in prints and pictures and developed their
usiness into a great music publishing house from 1779 onwards.
ikewise in the early 1770s Christoph Torricella, a Swiss, came to
ienna as an art-dealer, and in 1781 he also turned to music. The
istinction of actually issuing the first engraved music in Vienna
elongs to another immigrant, a Frenchman named Antoine
uberty, who left Paris in 1777, whence his publications had been
nported as early as 1770. A number of rival Austrian firms soon
orang up, all eager to profit from the great impetus to production
hich came from the so-called Viennese school of composers,
aydn, Mozart and Beethoven and their very prolific lesser con-
mporaries. Before long, because of sheer quantity, the average
andards of engraving and production became coarse and utili-
rian. There were naturally some honourable exceptions, both in
urope and elsewhere. The first music of substance to be engraved
Russia came from the St. Petersburg School of Mines, which was
ctive from 1789 to 1791. The finest production of its last year was
achal'noe upravlenie Olega, a drama with music by Sarti and others,
ell engraved in a distinctly French style. On the other hand, when
e process spread to the far east and reached India, where L.
/alckiers's *Collection of Twenty Four Hindoostanee and other Tunes* was
ngraved at Calcutta in about 1810, the standard of craftsmanship
as very low.

One specially interesting feature of the general dominance of
ngraving is the fact that it was not confined to the printing of parts.
here was also a steadily growing demand for scores. In about 1802,
eyel of Paris issued in pocket score an exceptionally well engraved
ollection of Haydn's string quartets and four of his symphonies as

well. The latter are probably the earliest scores of such works com
posed by any of the classical masters. Obviously, the engraved pla
provided a very convenient way to accommodate the increasir
number of staves required by the orchestral and operatic works
the early nineteenth century.

It was while engraving was at the height of its popularity tha
lithography was invented. For several reasons, it is unique amor
the various processes used for printing music. It is the only on
invented by one man whose name is known, who himself perfecte
its developments through several stages, and left a detailed accoun
of them. Unlike movable type and engraving, lithography was fron
its very beginning closely associated with music. During its first fiv
years, which might be termed the 'incunable' period, nearly half i
total production consisted of musical compositions.

Alois Senefelder was born at Prague in 1771, and died at Munic
in 1834. He tried to follow his father's profession as an actor, bu
met with little success. He then turned his hand to writing play
and, in 1796, while living in Ingolstadt (some fifty miles north o
Munich), he began to search for a method of printing them which
would be cheaper than engraving on copper. He chanced o
Solnhofen stone, on the polished surface of which any writing, don
in a special ink compounded of wax, soap and lampblack, left
sharp impression. The parts of the surface free from writing wei
easily etched away, and an impression was taken from the parts le
in relief, as from a woodblock.

At an early stage in his experiments, Senefelder left Ingolstad
and went to Munich, where he met Franz Gleissner, a composer o
slender talent and an instrumentalist in the Electoral band. Gleissne
played a doubly important part in developing Senefelder's exper
ments because he had the ability, which the inventor had not y
acquired, to write backwards, and because he provided him wit
music to publish. The first piece of any kind printed from etche
stone was a pianoforte composition by Gleissner entitled *Feldmars*
der Churpfalzbayer'schen Truppen. This was issued in 1796, apparent
in the later part of the year. (A few non-musical works followed
The earliest composition of importance so printed was Haydn
Trois sonates pour le forte piano, op. 37 (PL. XX) issued by the Munic
music publisher Falter early in 1797.

Printing from etched stone was not, however, true lithograph

This Senefelder discovered later in 1797 when he discontinued etching. As before, he wrote on the stone with his greasy ink, and then coated the surface with a mixture of water, acid and gum arabic. Finally he inked the whole, and the ink was absorbed solely by the writing. Thus an impression was left which could be taken directly from the surface of the stone. The basic principle was that one greasy material is attractive to another but is repelled by water.

This process which was perfected later in 1797, became widely known as 'chemical printing'. In its very nature, it is totally different from all other methods of printing music. The earliest composition, and the first work of any kind printed by it was a selection from *Die Zauberflöte*, arranged for string quartet by Franz Danzi, and also issued by Falter.[1] One great advantage of this process was its cheapness. On 19 May 1798 Falter, writing to Gombart, a music publisher in Augsburg, stated that the costs of printing chemical lithography were less than a quarter of those of engraving.

The third stage introduced a simplification whereby Senefelder discovered that, using his special ink, he could dispense with the need to write backwards, and write direct on the paper which could be pressed on the stone, so producing an impression in reverse. But the use of stones remained cumbrous and uneconomic because they tended to crack in the press. The next step was taken in 1805 when Senefelder began to adopt metal plates instead of stones, which made printing easier and quicker. Thus was established 'lithographic transfer', as the process was usually called – rather inaccurately, however, since stones were rarely used.

In various forms, lithographic music-printing spread quickly over Europe, mainly under the influence of Senefelder himself. In 1799 he went to Offenbach and met the music-publisher J. A. André. It was partly with the help of the relatives or employees of this influential man that Senefelder expanded his interests in the next few years. Late in 1800 he travelled to London, where Philipp André was living, and with his assistance secured the royal privilege for his invention in June 1801. (Its application to music was delayed until about 1806 when the Polyautographic Press was established under G. J. Vollweiler, a composer from Offenbach and a friend of the

---

[1] It is worth noting that the titlepage – or head-titles – of this and most other early lithographed music was still printed from engraved plates.

André family.) Early in 1802 Friederich André journeyed to Paris, began to print music by lithography and in the same year obtained a patent which he soon sold to a Madame Varnay. She set up at Charenton the 'imprimerie lithographique' and printed music in small quantities for publication by Madame Duhan in Paris. The management passed before long to Joseph Knecht, an employee of André sent from Offenbach. In 1803 Senefelder himself went to Vienna where he founded the famous 'Chemische Druckerei'.

Within a few years such major publishers as Schott of Mainz and Breitkopf of Leipzic – the latter with the personal co-operation of Senefelder – had adopted lithography for part of their production. In Italy Ricordi of Milan did likewise very soon after their foundation in 1808. The later development of the process in Italy was notable for its use in the publication of such very large works as the seven-volume *Raccòlta di musica sacra*, edited by Pietro Alfieri in 1841–46, and published at Rome by Pietro Pitarelli and his successors. At least eight handsome full scores of Rossini operas were printed between 1822 and c. 1830 by another Roman firm, Ratti, Cencetti & Co. Few works of such size were commercially printed by lithography elsewhere.

The visual effect of the best lithographed music is generally soft, fluent and clear: but the sharp immediacy of the best engraving is naturally lacking. A process so well suited to graphic art naturally led to a great increase in the use of pictorial titlepages and decorated borders. Illustration was occasionally attractively combined with the notes, as in some comic ballads published c. 1820 by a Birmingham lithographer named William Hawkes Smith, in which dancing figures and humorous scenes appear in the gap between each pair of staves and round the margins.

The relative simplicity of lithography sometimes attracted the composer strongly. In 1798 when Weber was twelve years old, he met Senefelder and frequented his workshop. The boy's keen observation, allied to his passion for all things mechanical, enabled him to learn the art so well that he lithographed his own opus 2, a set of pianoforte variations. Three years later, he wrote to Artaria 'I can engrave music on stone in a manner equal to the finest English copper plate engraving' – a remarkably confident statement. If a musician could not find a publisher for his music, transfer lithography enabled him to publish it himself. Few, however ndertook a task of such magnitude as did Wagner in 1845 when he wrote, in an astonishingly clear and regular hand, the 450 pages of *Tannhäuser* in full score, with a titlepage bearing the words 'Als Manuskript von der Handschrift der Componisten auf Stein gedruckt'.

Despite its adaptability, lithography enjoyed a limited success, and never became a serious rival to engraving. Indeed, in the early nineteenth century some big firms such as Breitkopf used both processes more or less simultaneously. Until the early 1850s, the engraved plate remained the medium from which a very high proportion of all music was printed. Most of the first editions of Beethoven, Schubert, Meyerbeer, Donizetti and Bellini were so produced. German craftsmanship led the way, and as the century wore on, engraving tools of German manufacture were those most widely employed.

Even now movable type was in small but steady demand. Breitkopf used it in 1801 to print the first edition of the full score of *Don Giovanni*, and of most of the cahiers of the so-called *Oeuvres complètes* of Haydn and Mozart, which were published between 1798 and about 1815. Attempts were still being made to improve the design of type, as for instance by Messrs. William Clowes when they devised a new and very pleasing fount for the copious musical supplements to *The Harmonicon*, the periodical published in London from 1823 to 1833. An unusual fount, with very thin note-stems and staves was developed by Garnier frères of Paris in 1843 and is found in that handsomely illustrated book *Chants et chansons populaires de la France*, edited by H. L. Delloye.

Type was most frequently used in two kinds of music-book, one sacred, the other secular. In many countries type was chosen to print the music in missals, hymnals, psalters and the like. Reprints were often called for, but it proved uneconomic to keep standing valuable type which was also liable to damage from repeated use. Therefore the stereotype process was widely favoured because it could be used on the speedy cylinder press. Movable music-type, which could be set together with the text-type, also proved ideal for printing short musical examples in works of musical theory and history and in programme notes. As musical education and enjoyment spread among the middle classes, such publications were in great demand.

The number of musical sorts cast in one fount in the m
nineteenth century exceeded 450, so that their use for printin
large score would have been impossibly slow and cumbrous. Mc
over even this quantity of sorts would have been inadequate
represent the full range and variety of expression demanded by
composers of the romantic era and later by virtuoso conduct
But the flexibility of the engraved plate could provide in almost a
format all that the most progressive musician could require. 7
skilful engraver employed by Guidi of Florence in 1860 produced
amazingly clear miniature full score of Rossini's *Guillaume Tell*,
using a plate only eighteen centimetres high which could nev
theless contain a maximum of twenty-two staves.

After about 1860, less and less music was printed direct fr
punched and engraved plates. This method was however retain
with an effect of simple dignity, to print many of the great editi
of the classics such as those issued by the German Bach Society,
German Handel Society, and the Purcell Society in Lond
Likewise, the transfer process, as it developed after Senefeld
death in 1834, had as its basis the plate, from which a print co
be taken and the image transferred to stone or zinc. (The origi
plate could be stored for future use.)

Later in the nineteenth century, the lithographic stone v
replaced by zinc and aluminium plates which could be used in co
junction with the rotary power press to give a greatly increa
speed of production. Further impetus has come from the applicati
of photographic and other mechanical techniques. The growth a
interaction of these processes belong to the history of music-printi
in its fifth century, and so lie beyond the scope of this book
In fine, economic pressure has combined with technology to facilit
the printing of very elaborate musical scores, but, as in earlier tim
technical gain was only won at the expense of variety and style.

Despite the touch of individuality introduced by the photograp
reproduction of manuscript scores (either in the hand of the co
poser or of a copyist), the once tasteful and diversified art of mus
printing has generally reached a level of uniformity more widespre
than at any time in its history. Failing a revolution in design
technique, the printed note now seems to have lost its forn
capacity to rival the range of processes and founts of type whi
were – and still are – available for the printing of books.

List of Selected Books and Articles

ᴏsson, Åke.   Die Literatur zur
hichte des Notendruckes.   In:
sala Universitets Årsskrift (Uppsala),
, 9, pp. 91-145

ᴋsDALE, A. Beverly.   The Printed
ᵉ. 500 years of music printing and
aving. (Catalogue of an exhibition
ᵉ Toledo Museum of Art.) Toledo,
, [1957]

ᴛᴋopf, Johann Gottlob Immanuel.
hricht von einer neuen Arten Noten
ᵣucken. Leipsic, 1755. (Facsimile,
ᵢ)

ᴍiri, Raffaele.   Simone Verovio da
ᵢogenbosc. In: 'Note d'archivio' per
oria musicale (Rome), 1933, p. 189,
., p. 66.

ᴛHL, Franz Maria.   Uebersicht der
ᵢg bestehenden, vollständigen
ᵢnabeln-Sammlung der Litho-
hie, etc. Munich, 1856

ᴛnier, Pierre.   Traité historique et
que sur l'origine et le progrès des
cterès de fonte pour l'impression
ᵢ musique. Paris, 1765

ʙle, William.   The History of
ic Engraving and Printing. London,
ᵢ. (Historically inaccurate: techni-
ᵧ good)

ᴠAERTS, Alphonse.   Histoire et
iographie de la typographie musicale
ᵢ les pays-bas. Anvers, 1880.

ᵢ, Sir Walter W.   'Notes on some
ᵧ Plays.' In: The Library (London),
4, June 1930, vol. II, pp. 44-56.
the dating of the fragmentary ballad
ᵗed by John Rastell and of his New
lude. See also Greg's Bibliography of
ᵢnglish Printed Drama, 1939, vol. I,
ᵢ)

HOPKINSON, Cecil.   A Dictionary of
Parisian Music Publishers, 1701-1950.
London, 1954

HUMPHRIES, Charles, and SMITH,
William C.   Music-Publishing in the
British Isles. London, 1953

LEBEAU, Elizabeth.   Les Debuts ignorés
de l'imprimerie lithographique. Charenton, Paris, 1802-1806. In: Bulletin de la
Société archéologique, historique 'Le
Vieux papier' (Auxerre), July 1952

LESURE, François.   'Pierre Haultin.' In:
Die Musik in Geschichte und Gegenwart
(Kassel), V, 1956, coll. 1827, 1828.
(Impugning Fournier's statement that
Haultin invented movable type for
printing music at one impression in 1525)

LUTHER, Wilhelm Martin.   'Notendruck. Von den Anfangen bis 1500.'
[With bibliography.] In: Die Musik in
Geschichte und Gegenwart (Kassel), IX,
1961, coll. 1667-1680

MEYER, afterwards MEYER-BAER, Kathi
[with Eva Judd O'Meara].   The Printing of Music 1473-1934. In: 'The
Dolphin' (New York), II, 1935,
pp. 171-207

MEYER, afterwards MEYER-BAER, Kathi.
Liturgical Music Incunabula. A des-
criptive catalogue. London, 1962

PATTISON, Bruce.   Notes on early Music
Printing. In: The Library (London),
ser. 4, vol. 19, March 1939, pp. 389-421

RIEMANN, Hugo.   Notenschrift und
Notendruck. In: Festschrift zur
50jährigen Jubelfeier des Bestehens der
Firma C. G. Röder. Leipsic, 1896

SARTORI, Claudio.   Bibliografia delle
opere musicale stamptati da Ottaviano
Petrucci. Florence, 1948

SARTORI, Claudio.   Dizionario degli editori musicali italiani. *Florence*, 1958

SCHAAL, Richard.   'Der Notendruck seit 1501.' [With bibliography.] In: *Die Musik in Geschichte und Gegenwart (Kassel)*, IX, 1961, coll. 1686-1695

SEIFFERT, Max.   Bildniszeugnisse des 16.Jahrhunderts für die instrumentale Begleitung des Gesanges und den Ursprung des Musik-kupferstiches. In: Archiv für Musikwissenschaft (*Leipsic*), I, 1918-19, pp. 49-67

SENEFELDER, Alois.   A Complete Course of Lithography . . . Translated from the original German, by A.S. [Adolph Schlichtegroll]. *London*, 1819

SQUIRE, William Barclay.   Notes on early Music Printing. In: Bibliograp (*London*), III, 1897, pp. 99-122

STEELE, Robert.   The Earliest Engli Music Printing. *London*, 1903

VOLKMANN, Ludwig.   J. G. I. Breitk und P. Fournier. In: Gutenberg Jahrbuch (*Mainz*), 1928, pp.118-14

VOLMAN, B. L.   Russkie pechatnuie notui XVIII veka. *Leningrad*, 1957

WAGNER, Carl.   Alois Senefelder. Se Leben und Wirken. *Leipsic*, 1914. (2 ed. 1943)

WALLNER, Bertha.   Musikalischer Denkmäler der Steinätzkunst. *Muni* 1912

Elegiaca harmonia ẽ qua in elegiacis miserisq; carminib.decantandis utimur:cuius numeri sunt tales.

Tempora labuntur tacitisq; senescimus annis

Et fugiunt freno non remorante dies

Prospera lux oritur:linguis animisq; fauete:

Nunc dicenda bona Sunt bona uerba die

---

de of twelue/the thyrde of eyght/the fourth of .iiij. as this fygure fheweth. ¶ Whan thefe accordes were foūdcypitago ras pat betyna mes. And fo þ be called iy nō bre double / be called iy fow/ nes Dyapafon And þ be called iy nōbre other halfe be called iy fowne Dya pente. And þ þ iy nōbre is cal/ led all ꝯ þ thyt

Duplex diapafon
Diateʃʃeron
Diapente
Diapafon

de dele/here iy fones Dyatefferon/ꝯ that þ iy nombres is called all ꝯ the eyghteth dele / here iy tewnes double Dyapafon. As iy melodye of one ſtrē ge/yf the ſtrynge be ſtreyned enlonge vpon the holowneſſe of a tree / ꝯ de/ parted euen a two by a brydge ſette there vnder iy eyther parte of þ ſtren ge/the fowne ſhall be Dyapafon/yf the ſtreng be ſtreyned ꝯ touched. And

PLATE VIa. Musical illustrations printed from wood-block. Nicol
Burtius: Musices opusculum. *Ugo Rugerius: Bologna*, 1487; sig. e 7 verso (20·5
14·5 cm)

❡ Et ſi puct⁹ nõ
poneret q̃lib₃ ma
ꭋia eēt pfecta et
ſcõa lõga eſſet al=
teꭋata exẽᵐ vt hic

❡ Simili modo oebet intelligi in q̃libet numeꭋo ter=
naꭋio vt ponũtur exempla

❡ Et ad habendũ₃ et cog=
noſcendũ₃ oifferentiã vni⁹
puncti ad alteruꭋ eſt ſcienð
ꝙ omnis punctus augmen=
tationis eſt ſituatus ſinc medio aliquo poſt figuram
imperfectaꭋ per ipm augmētataꭋ. ❡ Aullus pũct⁹

PLATE VIb. Musical illustrations printed from type by single impression.
Guillermus Guersoni: Utillissime musicales regule. *Michel Tholoze: P*
[c. 1496]; sig. d 7 recto (13·1 × 8·5 cm)

PLATE VII. A book of music entirely printed from wood-block. Martin Luther: Geystliche Lieder. *Valentin Babst: Leipsic*, 1545; [Psalmen] sig. B verso (15·7 × 9·6 cm)

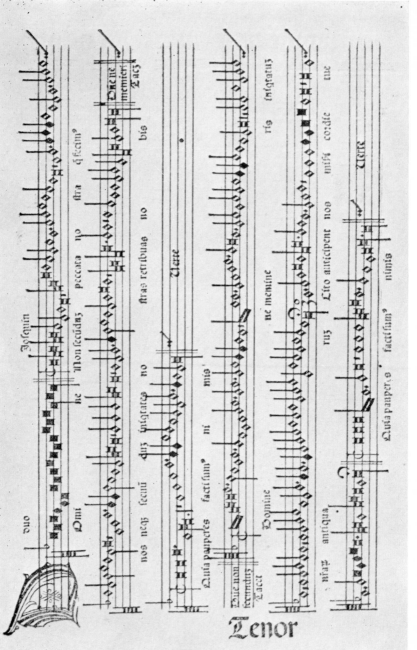

PLATE VIII.   Early mensural music printed from type by triple impression.   Motetti de passione, de cruce, de sacramento.

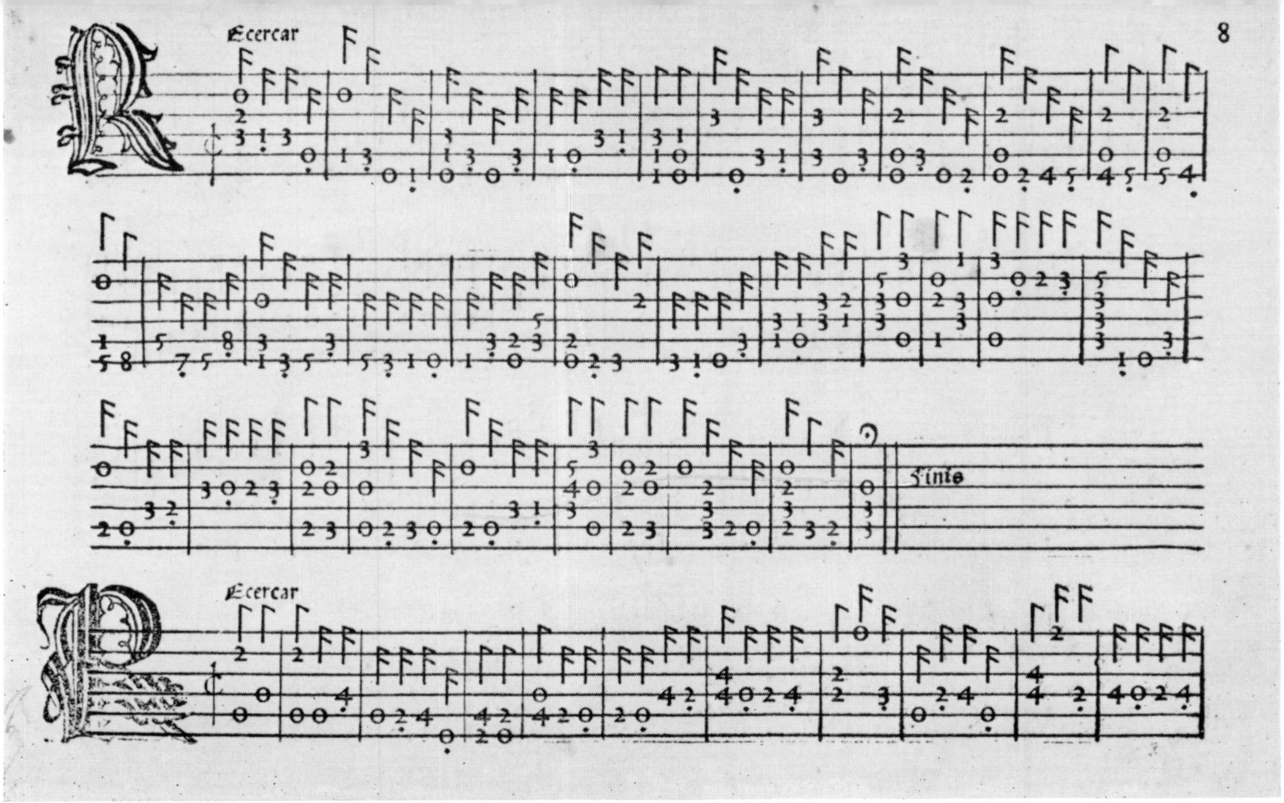

PLATE IX. An early printed tablature, printed from type by double impression. Joan Ambrosio Dalza: Intabolatura de liuto. Libro quarto. *Ottaviano dei Petrucci: Venice,* 1508; fol. 8 recto (15·6 × 22·9 cm)

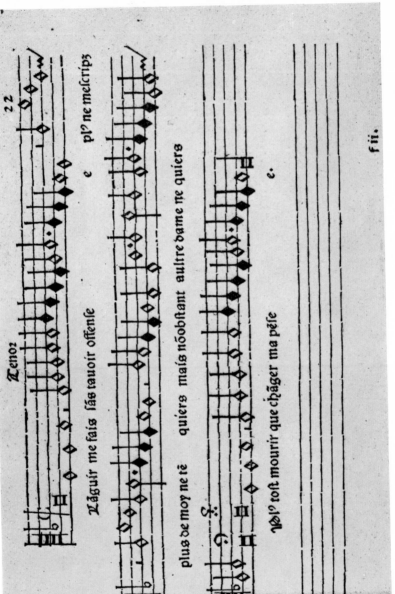

PLATE X. The earliest dated mensura music with text and notes printed from type by one impression. Chansons nou-

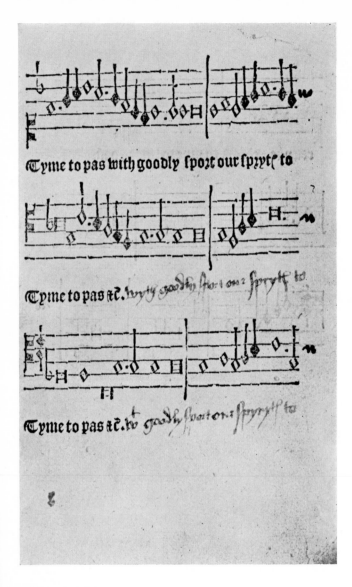

PLATE XI.   One of the two earliest pieces of mensural music printed in England,
he notes and underlaid text printed from type by one impression, with some of
he text added by hand.   [John Rastell: A New Interlude and a mery of
he Nature of the iiii Elements. *London*, c. 1527]; sig. E 5 recto (15·9 × 10·2 cm)

59

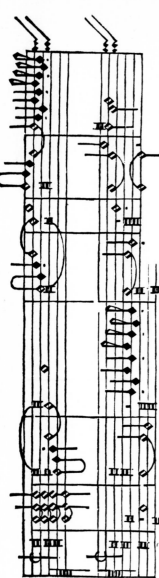

Recercare Secondo.

PLATE XIIa. Probably printed from metal block. Marco Antonio Cavazzoni: Recerchari, motetti, canzoni. Bernardus Vercellensis: Venice, 1523; sig. c 1 recto (13·6 × 20·1 cm)

PLATE XIIb. The earliest known musical illustration printed from an engraved plate, the text from type. Vicentio

Defcrittione de' 12. Tuoni, tratti dalla prima faccia del Dodicar- don del Gia- rcano, & dal 7. & del 28. del fecondo libro.

trarre il Nono dal Secondo : lafciando da parte come fi è detto, la diuifione harmonica del Diapafon che ferue al Quarto Modo, per non effene capace; fi come non è capace quella del Quinto dell'Aritmetica, fecondo che in quefto effempio fi può fenfatamente comprendere.

1	2	3	4	5	6	7	8	9	10	11	12
Dorio	Hypodorio.	Frygio	Hypofrygio.	Lydio	Hyplydio.	Mixolydio.	Hypomixolydio.	E olio.	Hypereolio.	Ionico.	Hypoionico.

I quali impedimenti cagionarono che piu oltre à maggior numero di Tuoni non fi paffaffe. dal che fi fa argumento, quanto male fia ftata intefa la cofa de Tuoni degli antichi Mufici da mo- derni; poi che fi fatte baie veramente, gli hanno dato occafione & impedite l'operationi loʒoʒ

Altro abufo de' moderni.

A devotional print, printed from a plate engraved by Jan Sadeler
er Martin de Vos, showing the Virgin and Child with St. Anne. The design
ludes a four-part motet, the earliest known composition printed by engraving.
rnelius Verdonck: Ave gratia plena. *Antwerp*, 1584 (25·9 × 19·6 cm)

PLATE XIV. One of the two earliest known books of music printed fr[ ]engraved plates.   Simone Verovio: Diletto spirituale.   Canzonette . . . c[ ]l'intavolatura del cimbalo et liuto.   *Rome*, 1586; fol. [17] verso (22·5 × 16·2 c[ ]

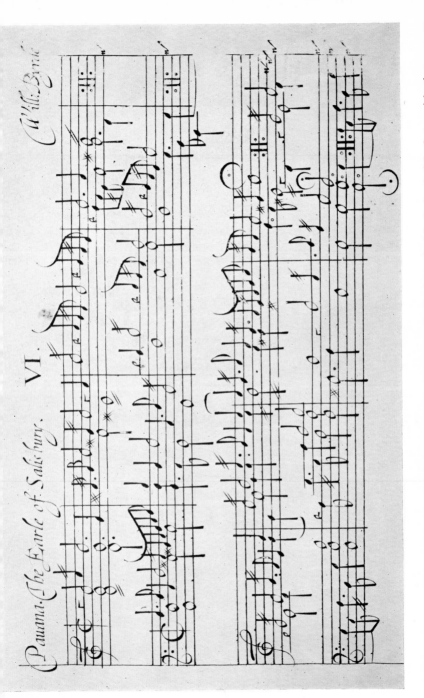

PLATE XV. The earliest English music printed from engraved plates. *Parthenia, or the Maydenhead of the first musicke that ever was printed for the Virginalls. Dorothy Evans: London,* [1612/13]; fol. [6] recto (18·7 × 12·4 cm)

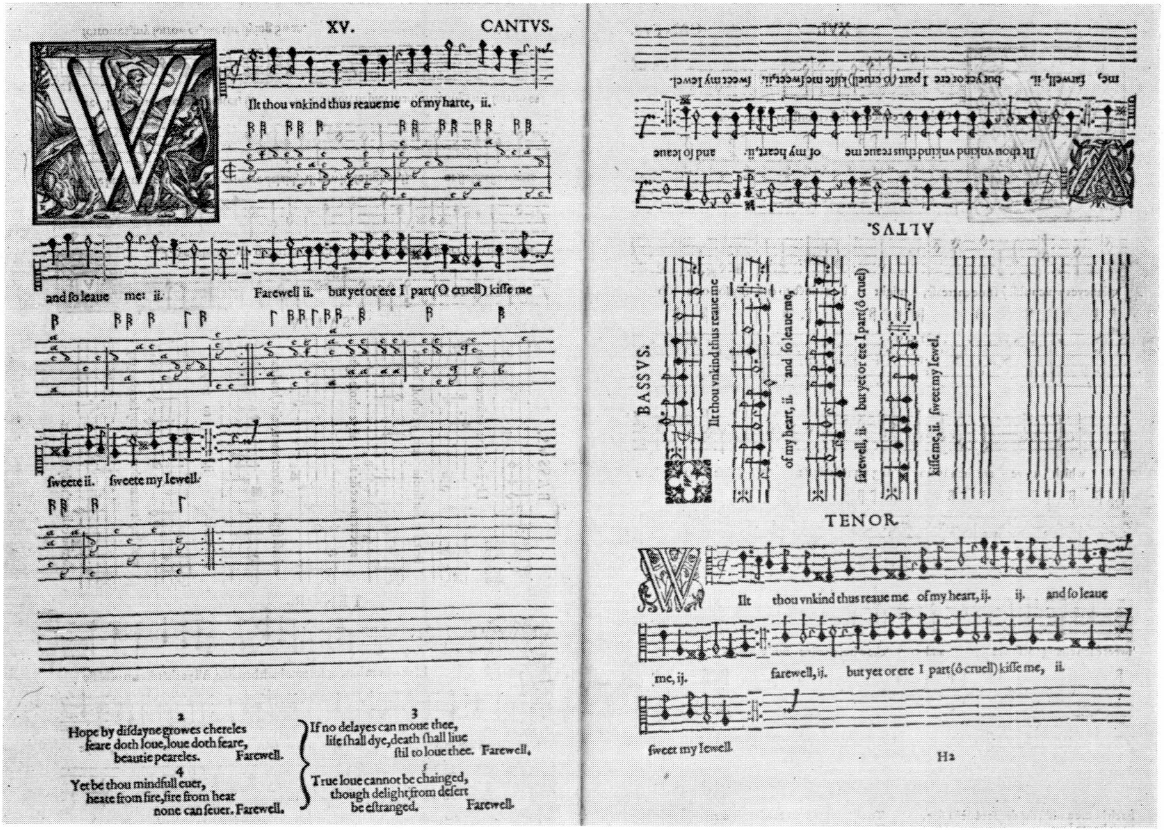

PLATE XVI.   Printed from type by one impression, each part facing the respective performer.   John Dowland:
The first Booke of Songes . . . Peter Short . . . London, 1597, sig. H1 verso, H2 recto (261.7 × 203 mm)

PLATE XVIII.   Printed from engraved plates.   George Bickham: The Musica Entertainer.   *Charles Corbett: London,* 1737, 38; vol. 1, pl. 21 (40·7 × 24·7 cm)

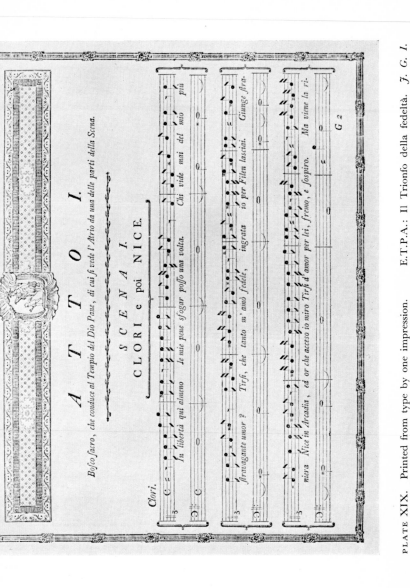

PLATE XIX. Printed from type by one impression. E.T.P.A.: Il Trionfo della fedeltà. J. G. I. Breitkopf : Leipsic, 1756; p. [27] (27·0 × 31·9 cm)

PLATE XX.   Printed by lithography from etched stone.   Franz Joseph Haydn: Trois sonates pour le forte piano.